The Color Wheel

Johns Hopkins: Poetry and Fiction

John T. Irwin, General Editor

The Color Wheel

Poems by Timothy Steele

The Johns Hopkins University Press

Baltimore and London

This book has been brought to publication with the generous
assistance of the Albert Dowling Trust.

Printed in the United States of America on acid-free paper

03 02 01 00 99 98 97   5 4 3 2

The Johns Hopkins University Press

2715 North Charles Street

Baltimore, Maryland 21218-4319

The Johns Hopkins Press Ltd., London

ISBN 0-8018-4951-9

ISBN 0-8018-4952-7 (pbk.)

Library of Congress Cataloging-in-Publication Data will be found at
the end of this book.

A catalog record for this book is available from the British Library.

For Terry Santos and Ruben Quintero

Contents

1

Aurora

Your sleep is so profound
This room seems a recess
Awaiting consciousness.
Gauze curtains, drawn around
The postered bed, confute
Each waking attribute —
Volition, movement, sound.

Outside, though, chilly light
Shivers a puddle's coil
Of iridescent oil;
Windows, sun-struck, ignite;
Doves strut along the edge
Of roof- and terrace-ledge
And drop off into flight.

And soon enough you'll rise.
Long-gowned and self-aware,
Brushing life through your hair,
You'll notice with surprise
The way your glass displays,
Twin-miniatured, your face
In your reflective eyes.

Goddess, it's you in whom
Our clear hearts joy and chafe.

Awaken, then. Vouchsafe
Ideas to resume.
Draw back the drapes: let this
Quick muffled emphasis
Flood light across the room.

A Shore

It's pastoral enough—the flat, slick sand;
The towel draped round the neck, as if a yoke;
The toppling waves; the sunset, as it smoulders
And drains horizonwards, fiery, baroque;
The young girl sitting on her father's shoulders,
Directing his attention here and there,
Her ankles held and her unpointing hand
Contriving a loose pommel of his hair.

Here strollers pass, pant legs rolled up like sleeves,
Shoes hanging over shoulders, laces tied,
While godwits—rapier bills upcurved—peruse
Bubbles beneath which burrowed sand crabs hide.
Though hardly anyone these days conceives
That this is where the known meets the unknown,
The ocean still transmits its cryptic news
By means of a conch's ancient cordless phone.

And night will put an end to pastorals.
A crescent moon will cup its darker sphere.
The waves will crash in foam and flood up through
The forest of the piles below the pier.
Alone, archaically, the sea will brew
Its sundry violence beyond the shore,
Beyond the sweeping beam, where heaving swells
Of kelp-beds wage titanic tugs-of-war.

For My Sister

A rainy evening's saturated boughs
Are blowing at the window; you address
A jigsaw on the carpet. Hard to piece
The landscape back together, piece by piece!
You lean upon one arm, and your head bows,
Legs folded in the island of your dress.

Pursed lips admitting puzzlement, you face
The possibilities that the hours open,
So calmly concentrating, I don't wonder
That the wall's grounded outlet, as if in wonder
Appears to watch. (See, its thrice-slotted face
Is looking on, astonished mouth wide open.)

Though time is shifting into overdrive,
And the years pass more quickly, even here,
It's not surprising that you've made a harbor
In this damp chilly evening, where you harbor
The sense not to be driven or to drive.
Patience itself will make the world cohere.

Cosmos

Arms branchingly uplifted,
Like candelabra-crazies,
They dominate the ground
That they were meant to border.
How lavishly they're drifted
With blooms like those of daisies;
How brightly they confound
The fact their name means order.

What hard spring storms they weathered.
Along with cyclamen,
They vivified the rose's
Contrasting pomp and pelf.
Now head-high, shaggily-feathered,
Their foliage heartens when
The lone daylily closes
By withering round itself.

When, drawing moth and bee,
They're summer-swayed and blent,
When each bloom's a free-standing
Botanic carousel,
A grand apostrophe
Is surely pertinent:
Your namesake is expanding;
Fair friends, do so as well.

Eros

By rights one should experience holy dread
At the young woman gowned in black chiffon
Who, at a mirror, slightly turns her head,
Large eyes intent, and puts an earring on.
One should fear redwoods where the sun sinks shafts
Of glowing light through dust-revolving drafts
And where the cyclist slimly coasts through trees
As she leans forward, her arms long and brown,
And gives her brakes a moderating squeeze.

Yet the soul loves the braided rope of hair,
The sense of heat and light, the cheek's faint flush.
Time blurs; nights end; one climbs a narrow stair,
The studio's warm, the city is a hush
Of streetlamps and the snow that, all night, falls.
But later when one rises and recalls
How, in the dark, the spirit clings and melts,
It is as if the ardent, giddy rush
Had happened, somehow, to somebody else.

Gently to brush hair from the sleeping face,
To feel breath on the fingers, and to try
To check joy in that intimate, small place
Where joy's own joyousness can't satisfy—
This is pain. This is power that comes and goes.

This is as secret as the fresh clean snows
Which, destitute of traffic to confess,
Will serve at dawn as witness to a sky
Withdrawing to its high blue faultlessness.

California Sea Lion

The waves wash in, old prankster, and they strand
Your carcass on the gentle slope of sand
Till other waves, out-draining, drag you back,
The great trunk of your body sleek and black.

Snout skyward and chest swelled and flippers out,
You doubtless honked the rival bulls to rout
Or flop-slid to the water from the rocks,
Inured to the cold rains of the equinox.

In frolic or some deadlier pursuit,
You'd porpoise through the swells and, diving, shoot
With tail-whipping fluidity and speed
Down chasms with their current-waving weed.

Now those same waters surge around your form;
They slick and shine the coat that kept you warm;
They roll and tug you as they slide away,
As if to try to coax you back to play.

Homage to a Carnegie Library

In the reading room
A boy takes notes
From a *World Book* volume.
His school report's
About the telescope
Or Alexander
Or (that old show-stopper)
The Venus flytrap.

Snow falling outside,
A radiator hisses;
Inquiries are whispered;
Someone coughs; a book closes
With an audible thump.
Newspapers on spindles
Hang, limp verticals,
In a rack by a lamp.

And the boy, determined,
With his pencil scratches
His notepad's green-lined
Yellow pages . . .
Companionable room,
In that early darkness
You stood in promise
Of a sunnier time.

From broad shallow shades,
The bulbs over the tables
Gloss the rich wood's
Grainy surfaces,
Though the dark grow deeper,
Though the boy discover
The streets all quiet
Through the homeward night.

Dependent Nature

The worker hovers where the jade plant blooms,
Then settles on a blossom to her taste;
Her furred and black-and-yellow form assumes
A clinging curve by bending from the waist.

So, too, the sweetpeas, climbing on their net,
Cast wire-wrapping tendrils as they flower,
Nor need they shield themselves from a regret
Of the dependent nature of their power.

They're spared the shrewd self-mockery of the sage
Attuned to limits and disparity.
They're spared the sad mirth serving those who gauge

The gap between the longed-for and the real,
Who grasp provisional joy, who must not be
Desolate, however desolate they feel.

Anecdote of the Sugar Bowl

Stern, hands on hips, the sugar bowl
Rebuked our lack of self-control
As we nine children kicked to cable
Intelligence beneath the table,
Bruising one another's shins
With these nonverbal bulletins.

As if a kind of referee,
Like Stevens' jar in Tennessee,
While coalitions came and went,
It was a stable referent
And from the chaos drew a meal
And brought our wilderness to heel.

I can't remember, looking back,
What led to this or that attack,
To blows I did or didn't strike.
I just recall it—matronlike
And arms akimbo, fixing me
With its fierce objectivity.

Her Memory of the Picnic

To finger-sponge crust crumbs of fruit meringue
(Grass prickling through the blanket-tablecloth);
To climb the shading oak; to roll and hang
Inverted from a branch, as if a sloth;
And, after dropping neatly from the branch,
To pull a cup off of a tube of cups;
To grab a towel hurriedly to stanch
A soda which, on opening, erupts—

This was to be there thirty years ago,
A time constrained and hurtful, yet the day
Now has the settled warmth of a tableau.
Cloud stacks stand whitely, farmlands stretch away,
While her two brothers, in a make-believe
World Series, wave their baseball gloves and run
About the meadow as they stab and heave
Each other blinding high-flies in the sun.

Her uncle, to distract and to compose
An argument between his daughters, lies
Upon his back and eye-catchingly blows
Smoke rings which grayly loosen as they rise.
Her parents will divorce within a year,
But neither fully grasps the crisis yet:
They kneel and wrap leftovers and appear
Absorbed in a congenial tête-à-tête.

And she can walk the meadow at her ease,
Switching the tall grass with an osier wand;
Can hear the white-throats in the woods reprise
The long rich notes with which they correspond;
Can spread and duck through a barbed wire fence;
Can sit on, horseback style, a fallen tree
While grasshoppers perform leaps so immense
They seem beyond the claims of gravity.

This idyll will be, she intuits, brief;
The fabric of the family will tear.
Yet this can't change the bittersweet belief
That pleasure's no less true for being rare;
Nor can it wholly undermine her sense
That though well-muscled follies hound and press,
What counts most is her own intelligence,
However cramped by grief and loneliness.

And even now, a cousin waves to her
And blows a summons through a trumpet-fist:
She's off to pick wildflowers and would prefer
To do so with a comrade botanist.
Investigating where the field declines
To marsh land, the two harvest or reprieve
Pinks, yellow bells, and long-spurred columbines
Till voices call them that it's time to leave.

Regretting his departure from the wild,
A stuffed bear's carried off; the sun moves west;
Her aunt holds on her hip her youngest child;
The slushed ice is dumped brusquely from its chest.
Caps are screwed back on thermoses and jars;
Her two ball-playing brothers pool their talents,
Porting between them a hamper to the cars,
Their outer arms held straining out for balance.

And if the meadows grow more darkly gold,
As though withdrawing now from living fact,
The blanket brushed, she and her mother fold
It up in squares increasingly compact.
She shinnies out the oak to roll and swing
A last time underneath the limb's rough girth,
Then hangs by hands, and lets go, fathoming
The distance of her drop back to the earth.

Luck

If we could be persuaded that luck is just
A species of good fortune which springs from chance,
    We'd feel less envy for the charmed life,
        Wouldn't regard with such mixed emotions

The friend who always lands in the perfect job,
Who finds support whenever he needs it most,
    Whose fairy godmother is clearly
        Sedulous, state-of-the-art, and doting.

But it is hard to credit fortuity.
Whatever happens to us is, we suspect,
    Part of a running commentary
        Upon our character. Were we rightly

Adjusted to the cosmos, we would be spared
The mean boss, the destructive relationship,
    So easy is it to imagine
        God's weighed our soul and has found it wanting.

Our earthly judges, meanwhile, are apt to muse,
Whenever sand is kicked in the blameless face,
    "Fate seems like such a nice boy; surely
        Something you did must have roused his ire."

Accorded such reflections, what can one do
But warmly shake the counseling hand and say,
    "Thanks so much for your insight; Job's own
        Comforters couldn't have been more helpful!"

These days I think that even the Calvinist
Must cease to worry whether or not he's graced
    And feel luck, like the rain in Matthew,
        Randomly falls on the just and unjust.

Insidious sad spectre who softly asks,
"Why aren't you famous, rich?" old careerist-priest,
    Enjoy your mansioned malversations.
        Henceforth, your servant intends an exit

Out through the avenue of the linden trees.
Albeit the Lord visit the fathers' sins
    Unto, yea, the fourth generation,
        Boughs dispatch leaves windward, willy-nilly.

Fae

I bring Fae flowers. When I cross the street,
She meets and gives me lemons from her tree.
As if competitors in a Grand Prix,
The cars that speed past threaten to defeat
The sharing of our gardens and our labors.
Their automotive moral seems to be
That hell-for-leather traffic makes good neighbors.

Ten years a widow, standing at her gate,
She speaks of friends, her cat's trip to the vet,
A grandchild's struggle with the alphabet.
I conversationally reciprocate
With talk of work at school, not deep, not meaty.
Before I leave we study and regret
Her alley's newest samples of graffiti.

Then back across with caution: to enjoy
Fae's lemons, it's essential I survive
Lemons that fellow Angelenos drive.
She's eighty-two; at forty, I'm a boy.
She waves goodbye to me with her bouquet.
This place was beanfields back in '35
When she moved with her husband to L.A.

Cory in April

Left punch-drunk from a decade in the ring,
He spends his noondays in the local park,
Gazing unbitterly into the void
Of being forty-two and unemployed.
The boy who, pumping easily on a swing,
Sweeps back and forth in an unvarying arc;

The trees with their new wealth of foliage,
Black roots exposed, trunks rough with thick bark pleats;
The Saint Bernard patrolling a stone walk
On which a hopscotch grid is sketched in chalk—
These things might drive another man to gauge
Life's quaint, sure sturdiness by his defeats.

But Cory can't weigh loss, though he'll relate,
Gripping a paper-bagged pint by the neck,
How with a Cuban middleweight he starred in
Some legendary bloodbath in the Garden:
My legs were dead, one eye was swollen shut,
But I kept coming back up off the deck

And finally TKO'd him in the twelfth.
Then he'll lean back and speak of lesser wars,
Not sad at what he has become, but sad
Only at something which he never had:
A few years at the top—brief spendthrift wealth,
Limousines, nightclubs, clothes from fancy stores.

The strong are skilled at learning how to house
The hurts they suffer, but it's they at length
Who most remind us of fragility.
A mother, at a stroller, expertly
Adjusts the collar of her baby's blouse,
While the child grips, a parody of strength,

The stroller's crossbar in her pudgy fists.
Two girls, each in a blazer and tartan skirt,
Play marbles in a circular patch of dust,
Their contest overseen by a black bust
(A square-jawed colonial governor) which resists,
Surely and sternly, weather, time, and dirt.

Not so with Cory who, as day wears on,
Will grow more querulous, now coughing out
His harsh, sweet-liquored cough, now babbling of
Some girl and what he once went through for love,
Now staring at the far side of the lawn,
As if adrift in sun-dazed seas of doubt.

And should the passer-by discriminate
In him or how he sits fixed at his station
A hardihood at bay, a more exact
Perception would be of a brutal fact
On which not even he'd dare speculate,
Were he at all inclined to speculation.

Practice

The basketball you walk around the court
Produces a hard, stinging, clean report.
You pause and crouch and, after feinting, swoop
Around a ghost defender to the hoop
And rise and lay the ball in off the board.
Solitude, plainly, is its own reward.

The game that you've conceived engrosses you.
The ball rolls off; you chase it down, renew
The dribble to the level of your waist.
Insuring that a sneaker's tightly laced,
You kneel — then, up again, weave easily
Through obstacles that you alone can see.

And so I drop the hands I'd just now cupped
To call you home. Why should I interrupt?
Can I be sure that dinner's ready yet?
A jumpshot settles, snapping, through the net;
The backboard's stanchion keeps the ball in play,
Returning it to you on the ricochet.

Decisions, Decisions

Free will being, it is commonly agreed,
A glory of the species, why balk at choice
Or, nettled and perplexed by doubt, resort
To heads-or-tails or petals of a flower?
Whence come these indecisions, abdications?

Riding the bus home on wet nights, one sees
The boarded store-fronts, the shapes slumped in doorways;
The rain blows curtains of illusory silver
Under the streetlights. In God alone, intention
And execution are simultaneous.

In God alone can choice be sure it *is* choice.
The contingent spirit must whistle in the dark,
Bucking itself up, choosing, choosing, knowing
That time may claim those choices with its own
Inevitable air of history.

Georgics

The heavy Holsteins, patterned white and black,
The milder Jerseys, in fawn-colored coats,
Would graze the river meadows, green beneath
The clouds' immense, white, forward-leaning floats.

And when the air was heavy they lay down,
An augury, or so folk wisdom held:
The afternoon was building to a storm;
By nightfall we would all be wetly shelled.

They plodded to the barn at milking time;
We'd shoulder and push back the sliding door.
The border collie yapping at their heels,
Their hooves clopped in across the concrete floor.

And so they had their few days in the sun —
Then, long months stanchioned in a filthy stall,
Consuming a grim winter's worth of hay
And destined to be slaughtered after all.

It's futile to indulge in litanies
About the cruelties of man, and yet
Those creatures served us, and it's hard to think
Without shame or a spasm of regret

Of how they grazed, contented, by the river
And lifted us their huge, attentive eyes
Or, forelegs in the water, bowed to drink
And shook their broad flat foreheads free of flies.

Beatitudes, While Setting Out the Trash

The sparrow in the fig tree cocks his head
And tilts at, so to speak, his daily bread
(The sunset's stunningly suffused with gold).
A squirrel on the lawn rears and inspects
A berry in its paws and seems to hold
The pose of a Tyrannosaurus Rex.

The clothesline's plaids and stripes perform some snaps;
A page of blown newspaper smartly wraps
A fire hydrant in the day's events;
And there's engaging, if pedestrian, song
Ringing its changes from a chain-link fence
A boy with a backpack walks a stick along.

I park my rattling dolly at the curb
And set the trash among leaves gusts disturb.
Then, hands tucked in my sweatshirt's pocket-muff,
A mammal cousin of the kangaroo,
I watch my breath contrive a lucent puff
Out of lung-exhalated CO_2.

Small breath, small warmth, but what is that to me?
My steps re-traced, the bird's still in his tree:
He grooms, by nuzzling, a raised underwing;
He shakes and sends a shiver through his breast,
As if, from where he perches, counseling
That *Blessed are the meek*, for they are blest.

2

Takeoff

Our jet storms down the runway, tilts up, lifts:
We're airborne, and each second we see more—
Outlying hangars, wetlands with a pond
That flashes like sheened silver and, beyond,
An estuary and the frozen drifts
Of breakers wide and white along a shore.

One watches, cheek in palm. How little weight
The world has as it swiftly drops away!
How quietly the mind climbs to this height
As now, the seat-belt sign turned off, a flight
Attendant rises to negotiate
The steep aisle to a curtained service bay.

Portrait of the Artist as a Young Child

Your favorite crayon is Midnight Blue
(Hurrah for dark dramatic skies!)
Though inwardly it makes you groan
To see it like an ice-cream cone
Shrink with too zealous exercise.

But soon you're offering for review
Sheets where Magenta flowers blaze.
And here's a field whose mass and weight
Incontrovertibly indicate
You're in your Burnt Sienna phase.

Long may you study color, pore
Over Maroon, Peach, Pine Green, Teal.
I think of my astonishment
When I first saw the spectrum bent
Around into a color wheel,

A disc of white there at the core,
The outer colors vivid, wild.
Red, with its long wavelengths, met
With much-refracted violet,
And all with all were reconciled.

When I look past you now, I see
The winter amaryllis bloom
Above its terra-cotta pot
Whose earthen orange-apricot
Lends warmth to the entire room.

And cherry and mahogany
Introduce tones of brown and plum;
While by the hearth a basket holds
Balls of yarn—purples, greens, and golds
That you may wear in years to come.

Yet for the moment you dispense
Color yourself. Again you kneel:
Your left hand spread out, holding still
The paper you'll with fervor fill,
You're off and traveling through the wheel

Of contrasts and of complements,
Where every shade divides and blends,
Where you find those that you prefer,
Where being is not linear,
But bright and deep, and never ends.

Advice to a Student

Frame your excuse, when your work is late,
 By Aristotelian laws.
It is essential that your fate
 Derive from a credible cause.
Fill the instructor with pity and fear:
 You mustn't be afraid
To fabricate deaths of the near and dear
 If this will serve your grade.

Gods-from-machines won't help you pass.
 Only the inept say,
As I was bringing my essay to class,
 Boreas blew it away.
Don't get too tricky; unify;
 Keep your tale under control;
Make each part of the alibi
 Suit the organic whole.

Always present yourself as one
 Who, neither saint nor god,
Didn't quite get the assignment done,
 Being tragically flawed.
Art judges not only deeds, but intentions;
 Much is allowed to youth.
You may win pardon by means of inventions
 That supersede the truth.

On Wheeler Mountain

If sometimes, as we call across the wood
To keep track of each other's whereabouts,
I'm slow to answer, be it understood
That an opposing boulder or steep hollow
Compels me to assess the course I follow
And for a moment plunges me in doubts.

Bear with me. With a shrug, adjust your pack.
Observe a jay, wings folded and severe,
Perched like a scholar, hands behind his back.
Or listen, on the quiet forest floor,
To winds that comb the hardwoods to a roar
Flowing across the upper atmosphere.

And, even as that sound subsides, remark
Different distractions: dangly-headed sedges;
A birch tree's tattered latitudes of bark;
A steep brook, plashing down its landing shelves,
Whose running margins seem to race themselves
When they slide over wider, flatter ledges.

Such beauties are the solitary sort?
You needn't, as you note them, feel alone.
From a log nearby, with a sharp report,
I'll snap a stick to help me as I climb.
And, when you call my name a second time,
I'll holler back an answer with your own.

Education in Music

Music meant turmoil put to rout,
Obstacles gaily overcome.
The sofa served for stretching out,
While fish in the aquarium
Exhibited a feathery speed
Among branched coral; deeply swayed,
The arms of a histrionic weed
Conducted what the stereo played.

The same engaging music spoke
Of the external, foggy night.
Richly a cello would evoke
Streetlamps wearing haloed light,
A park where footprints wetly blurred
In the mist-silvered grass they crossed,
Front doors whose fanlights registered
Ghost numbers in a stenciled frost.

Hands knit behind my head, my gaze
Conversing mildly with the ceiling,
I'd hear the aging Haydn praise,
By reconciling, thought and feeling,
His mind determined and at rest,
Yet scoring, too, a darker theme:
Less lucky dreamers, who've possessed
No governing, absorbing dream.

Past, Present, Future

Coming out of the local corner market,
I hear a screech of tires from the intersection.
It's the familiar drama: motorists
At loggerheads. One wants to make a left turn;
The other, with the right of way, takes umbrage
At the maneuver. They exchange the finger
And, were they armed, they'd probably trade bullets.
They lean on their respective horns, inducing
Cars jamming up behind them to do the same.

Granted, there's nothing new about the fatal
Concurrence of bad manners and bad driving:
The greatest of Greek tragedies in essence
Treats the effects of Laius's refusal
Courteously to yield to Oedipus
At that ambiguous junction of three highways.
Still, the world's population will soon reach
Eight billion souls, all wanting to be heard
And many fancying that cars and Uzis
Are proper instruments of self-expression.

With a concluding burst of profanity,
The motorists compose their differences.
A workman at the curb, having observed
The contretemps, shakes a regretful head.

People, he says to me as I pass by,
Cradling my groceries; then he lays his belly
Back on his jackhammer, and resumes drilling.

In Passing

The merest glance in passing comprehended
The jogger stretching at the leaning tree.
Head bowed between her arms, her arms extended,
She bent first one and then the other knee,
And looked as if engaged with main and might
In an attempt to push the tree upright.

The tree of course remained obliquely rooted,
Its flaky trunk a mottled reddish-brown.
A pair of brightly speckled starlings bruited
Their gossip through the airy open crown.
Attention turned, unable to detect
How clear the scene would grow in retrospect.

Hair gathered in a ponytail behind her,
The figure leaned in toward the Chinese elm
Which, mirroring her posture there, defined her,
As she did it, though not to overwhelm,
But rather to endeavor to enlist
Support from what had power to resist.

The Library

Emerging through the automatic doors,
I feel the Santa Anas' gusting heat.
It's five o'clock. The grainy sunlight pours
Through eucalypti whose peeled bark strips beat
The trunks to which they cling like feeble sleeves.
The campus lawns are eddyings of leaves
Viewed by day's milky, unassertive moon.
The sculpture garden has a recessed seat.
I take it, thinking of the afternoon

And of the library. Cultural oasis?
Few would object to its conserving aims.
Still, tracking books by way of data bases,
I feel I'm playing Faustian video games.
And jotting notes down from computer screens,
I doubt our armories of ways and means:
Whether in books or trusted to a disc,
The written record may, as Plato claims,
Subvert and put our memory at risk.

Yet books consoled me when I was a child,
And seeing words and software joined and sync-ed,
Even philosophers might be beguiled.
And if I relish verses nimbly linked,
Here flowing, there concluded with a twist,
It was a Greek librarian-archivist
Who had an odd pedantic inspiration—

Make prose and poems textually distinct —
And first gave lyric measures lineation.

Banners on the Art Gallery's facade
Ripple and flap; in a collegial wrath,
Two birds dispute rights to a carob pod;
A puffed-up brown bag somersaults a path
Where Rodin's *Walker* makes his headless stride.
Leaves spin up into coilings and subside.
This windy much-ado, arising from
The desert could well serve as epitaph
For Alexandria, Rome, Pergamum —

For all the ancient libraries whose collections
Have vanished in a mammoth wordless void.
And though I have the evening clouds' confections,
Thoughts of the art and science thus destroyed
Leave me a little empty and unnerved.
The consolation? Some things were preserved,
Technology now limits what is lost,
And learning, as it's presently deployed,
Is safe from any partial holocaust.

I could construct a weighty paradigm,
The Library as Mind. It's somehow truer
To recollect details of closing time.
Someone, at slotted folders on a viewer,

Tucks microfiche squares in their resting places;
Felt cloth's drawn over the exhibit cases;
The jumbled New Book Shelves are set in shape;
The day's last check-outs are thumped quickly through a
Device that neutralizes tattle-tape.

And shelvers, wheeling booktrucks through the stacks,
Switch lights off at the ends of empty aisles;
Jaded computer terminals relax;
Above lit spaces of linoleum tiles,
The hitching-forward minute hands of clocks
Hold vigil still, but a custodian locks
The main door, and the last staff members go
Home to their private lives and private trials.
Still ovenish, the Santa Anas blow

The leaves about in rustling shifting mounds;
The long, rust-colored needles pine trees shed
In broom-straw trios strew the walks and grounds;
Winding, as though along a corkscrew's thread,
A squirrel has circled down a sycamore.
The frail must, in fair times, collect and store,
And so, amid swirled papery debris,
The squirrel creeps, nosing round, compelled to hoard
By instinct, habit, and necessity.

Walking Her Home

Exhilarated by the wet and wind,
He may have been too quick and droll by half,
But she was at his side and capuchinned,
And he felt cheered that he could make her laugh,
As gusts splashed water-droplets from the trees;
Though other nights would sink him to a chair,
His head bowed and his elbows on his knees,
His hands plunged in the darkness of his hair,
He folded back her hood and kissed her brow.
And that much she would never disavow.
They walked on, trading jest and anecdote;
The street was plastered leaves and chestnut burs;
His hands deep in the pockets of his coat,
She tightly hugged his arm in both of hers.

Joseph

The fridge clicks, hums; light flows across
Cold sleeping tiles, and I survey
Red chilies, lime juice, tartar sauce —
Things I can't use or throw away
And which, some hours from morning, wear
An aspect of profound despair.

A glass of milk? Perhaps some food?
I draw a carton from the back.
Ranged on the wall by magnitude,
Knives gleam on their magnetic rack.
Novitiate-like, I stand before
The cylinder of white I pour.

What woke me? Was it that I sensed
The far drone of a passing plane?
I drink, then lean my head against
The chill damp of the windowpane,
And all the while the ticking clock's
Like a plain, baffling paradox.

Each quick, clenched moment's like the next.
Yet time yields shape and history.
I think — disquieted, perplexed —
How Joseph knelt at Pharaoh's knee
As he leaned from his throne to hear
The meaning of his dreams made clear

And luminous, for once, with hope.
When I look up I see in space
The moon as through a telescope:
Vague winds cross, streamingly, its face,
Remote and icy and antique,
And to its light I whisper, Speak.

A miracle! we say, astonished at life,
    And, given time, our briefcase in hand,
We hurry to work and savor clattering
    Through the makeshift tunnel that detours
The sidewalk out around a construction site,
    The fresh plywood springy underfoot.

Savor, too, sitting at the desk, with the phone
    Tucked aside the cheek, in the manner
Of a virtuoso with a violin;
    Savor the one feeling comment slipped
Into the otherwise official report:
    Jones says that if we hire her, it will
Be over his dead body, and I suggest
    We tell him these terms are agreeable.

Despite all this, no prevenient care delays
    The vigil by the hospital bed,
The loved face relaxing towards a real death, while
    In the night outside, a gusting wind
Shudders stop signs and sets traffic lights swinging
    Over deserted intersections.

And if, in that bleak attendance, one hope stirs
    It is that, at time's end, the First Cause

Will gather back to itself its poor effects.
  Until then we attempt to preserve
Something from the experiential flux. We set
  Peat pots by a window or recall
A woman coaxing, with a fork, a waffle
  From the iron's sticky upper grid
Or imagine the girl who, a century back,
  Standing behind her seated sister,
Takes up the lustrous wealth of dark tresses, draws
  Them into three plaits, and starts braiding.

Hortulus

To thwart a rear attack, a bird backs under
The wheelbarrow tire's curving shelter, while
Her suitor squawks and waves his wings about
In angry-plaintive-pleading-lover style.
Too great an ardor is a common blunder:
She sees him through an unromantic lens
And answers his hysteria with doubt
And all but asks him, *Can't we just be friends?*

The plants are luckier; fragile or strong,
They court each other in a world of green
And, when they need assistance in a suit,
Repose trust on an insect go-between.
A wasp, its trailing stork-legs thin and long,
Surveys sprawled foliage whose gaps disclose
The yellow trumpet flower, announcing fruit,
That a zucchini wears upon its nose.

The bird has no such help and can't entice
His love from her protective overhang;
He takes up, following a wide excursus
Around her, the main theme of his harangue.
One thinks, *Woo clemently.* Beyond advice,
He flies off to a plum tree and receives
A limb's support and shamelessly rehearses
Plaints to a captive audience of leaves.

Long Paces

We'd not have guessed that we'd be heartened so
To see this snowshoe rabbit, months from snow,

Come from the woods with that shy tread of his,
Drawn by our bushy rows of lettuces,

His summer coat all rich soft grays and browns,
His feet as overstated as a clown's.

How delicate he is: he holds no brief
For this or that variety of leaf,

But tries each, crouching as a cat will do
Before a dinner bowl and, when he's through,

Slips back across the grasses gingerly
(Binoculars enable us to see

The crickets that his cautious lopings flush)
And vanishes into the underbrush.

Woman in a Museum

You sit, suspending your critique
Of Venuses and nymphs at play,
While a few scattered strollers creak
Slowly across the floor's parquet.

Beside you on the bench, your purse
(Capacious well-worn leather) shows
A slumped, collapsed look. You, no worse
For touring, strike a fresher pose—

On your crossed legs your forearms crossed.
Your blond hair, in a single fold
Over your shoulder, makes a glossed
And negligent descent of gold.

And though a grace so natural
Seems something only art supplies,
You now, with a distracted smile,
Among the static beauties, rise.

Vermont Spring

for T.G. on his 60th birthday

The woods enclose a pond where a low dock
Extends out with a buffer zone of tires;
The water's surface smokily suspires;
A woodpecker imparts a hollow knock
To the decayed and bleached spar of a tree.
If April mixes memories and desires,
Here it blends beauty with austerity.

Damp gusts can find no foliage to tremble.
And yet the forest, leafless, thus allows
White trilliums to bloom beneath its boughs.
The bracket mushrooms on the trees resemble
Mussels attached to pilings of a pier;
An upstream beaver having built his house,
His brook's diminished to a trickle here.

Above his dam, though, waters rush and braid
Around projecting rocks, while young ferns lift
Curled, seahorse heads and tentatively shift
In air that summer will transform to shade,
As time will deepen talent into art.
Lucky the man who, coming to that gift,
Retains this vernal tang of mind and heart.

December in Los Angeles

The tulip bulbs rest darkly in the fridge
To get the winter they can't get outside;
The drought and warm winds alter and abridge
The season till it almost seems denied.

A bright road-running scrub jay plies his bill,
While searching through the garden like a sleuth
For peanuts that he's buried in the soil:
How different from the winters of my youth.

Back in Vermont, we'd dress on furnace vents.
A breakfast of hot cereal—and then
We'd forge out to a climate so intense
It would have daunted Scott and Amundsen.

I'd race down icy Howard Street to catch
The school bus and pursue it, as it roared
Up Union, my arms waving, pleading, much
To the amusement of my friends on board.

But here I look out on a garden, whose
Poor flowers are knocked over on their side.
Well, stakes and ties will cure them of the blues
(If not the winds) and see them rectified.

And in the shower is a pail we use
To catch and save the water while it warms:
I fetch and pour it on the irises
And hope this winter will bring drenching storms.

Youth

A dead oak's branches hold a nest,
Abandoned now, that ospreys built.
He wades the river; slow clouds spread
At each step from the bottom's silt.
Or, his shirt bunched beneath his head,
He drowses as the breeze falls slack,
And feels the grass he lies on pressed
In complex patterns on his back.

Though summer seems to pause with its
Hypnotic sluggishness and drouth,
Downstream a railway bridge extends
Across the estuary's mouth;
And, while the sliding water blends
Mercurial, flashing, glob-like fires,
Above the bridge a lineman sits
High in his seat-sling, working wires.

Pacific Rim

Unsteadily, I stand against the wash
Flooding in, climbing thigh, waist, rib cage. Turning,
It sweeps me, breaststroking, out on its swift
Sudsy withdrawal. Greenly, a wave looms;
I duck beneath its thundering collapse,
Emerging on the far side, swimming hard
For the more manageable, deeper waters.
How the sea elevates! Pausing to tread it
And feather-kicking its profundity,
The swimmer wears each swell around his neck,
And rides the slopes that heave through him,
The running valleys that he sinks across,
Part of the comprehensive element
Washing as well now the Galápagos,
The bay at Wenchow, the Great Barrier Reef.

Why, then, this ache, this sadness? Toweled off,
The flesh is mortified, the small hairs standing
Among their goose bumps, the teeth chattering
Within the skull. A brutal century
Draws to a close. Bewildering genetrix,
As your miraculous experiment
In consciousness hangs in the balance, do
You pity those enacting it? The headlands'
Blunt contours sloping to the oceanside,

Do angels weep for our folly? Merciful,
Do you accompany our mortality
Just as, low to the water, the pelican
Swiftly pursues his shadow down a swell?

Acknowledgments

Grateful acknowledgment is made to the following magazines, in whose pages some of the poems in this collection first appeared: *Crosscurrents, The Formalist, Gramercy Review, Greensboro Review, Hellas, Jacaranda Review, New Criterion, New Republic, Numbers* (England), *PN Review* (England), *Poetry Durham* (England), *Sequoia, Shenandoah, Southwest Review, Threepenny Review, Yale Review, Zyzzyva.* "The Library," "Eros," "December in Los Angeles," and "Hortulus" initially appeared in *Poetry*, copyright 1983, 1985, 1992 by the Modern Poetry Association.

Certain poems also appeared in the following chapbooks, anthologies, or festschriften: *Beatitudes* (Child Okeford, Dorset: Words Press, 1988), *Celebrations at Sixty for Turner Cassity*, edited by R. L. Barth (Florence, Ky.: Robert L. Barth Press, 1989), *The Direction of Poetry*, edited by Robert Richman (Boston: Houghton Mifflin, 1988), *A Few Friends: Poems for Thom Gunn's Sixtieth Birthday* (Walkerton, Ont.: Stonyground Press, 1989), *A Garland for Harry Duncan* (Austin: W. Thomas Taylor, 1989), *A Garland for John Finlay*, edited by David Middleton (Thibodaux, La.: Blue Heron Press, 1990), *A New Geography of Poets*, edited by Edward Field, Gerald Locklin, and Charles Stetler (Fayetteville: University of Arkansas Press, 1992), *Nine Poems* (Florence, Ky.: Robert L. Barth Press, 1984), *The Uncommon Touch*, edited by John L'Heureux (Stanford: Stanford Alumni Association, 1989).

The author thanks California State University, Los Angeles, for a Creative Leave that enabled him to finish this collection.

Born in 1948 in Burlington, Vermont, Timothy Steele received his B.A. from Stanford and his Ph.D. from Brandeis. He is the author of two previous collections of poems, *Uncertainties and Rest* (1979) and *Sapphics against Anger and Other Poems* (1986), as well as a book of literary criticism, *Missing Measures: Modern Poetry and the Revolt against Meter* (1990). His honors include a Guggenheim Fellowship, a Peter I. B. Lavan Younger Poets Award from the Academy of American Poets, the Los Angeles PEN Center's Literary Award for Poetry, and a Commonwealth Club of California Medal for Poetry. Currently, he lives with his wife in Los Angeles and is a professor of English at California State University, Los Angeles.

This book was typeset in Monotype Centaur
by the designer, Ann Walston.
It was printed by Thomson-Shore, Inc.
on 60-lb. Glatfelter Supple Opaque Recycled.

Library of Congress Cataloging-in-Publication Data

Steele, Timothy.
    The color wheel / Timothy Steele.
            p.   cm. — (Johns Hopkins, poetry and fiction)
    ISBN 0-8018-4951-9 (alk. paper). — ISBN 0-8018-4952-7
(pbk. : alk. paper)
    I. Title.   II. Series.
PS3569.T33845C65   1994
813'.54—dc20   94-15394

CPSIA information can be obtained at www.ICGtesting.com
Printed in the USA
LVOW10s1216021214

416604LV00007B/172/A

9 780801 849527